Accele
Learning

Proven Advanced Scientific Strategies and Techniques for Speed Reading, Comprehension and Memorization. Watch Your Productivity Skyrocket (Memory Training)

By

Jimmie Powell

TABLE OF CONTENT

INTRODUCTION 7

CHAPTER 1: THIS BOOK IS FOR WHOM? 12

CHAPTER 2: PREPARING TO LEARN 17

What Exactly is Learning..19

How Memory Plays a Role..21

How to View Failure 21

Knowledge, Understanding, Wisdom: What's the Difference?...26

Preparing the Mind 30

Human attention span:..31

Learning over short bursts of time 34

Surface learning vs. Deep learning...35

Concepts before Facts, Understanding before Memory...............36

Preparing the Heart 38

Preparing the Environment...40

CHAPTER 3: YOUR LEARNING ARSENAL...42

The Brain - How does it Work?..42

The Reptilian Brain 44

The Mammalian Brain 45

The Thinking Brain 47

The Two Minds 48

Intelligence - What is it, really? 51

Multiple Intelligences 53

Brain Waves 56

CHAPTER 4: YOUR MEMORY 61

The Forgetting Curve 64

Memory Retention 65

Five Types of Memory 66

How Emotions Play a Role 70

Use It or Lose It 72

Photographic Memory 73

CHAPTER 5: SIX STEPS TO FASTER LEARNING 75

Step 1: Motivating the Mind 78

Step 2: Acquiring the Information 83

Step 3: Searching Out the Meaning 92

Step 4: Triggering the Memory 94

Step 5: Exhibiting What You Know 100

Step 6: Reflection 103

CHAPTER 6: ALTERNATIVE LEARNING......... 105

Engaging the Mind..105

Master the Concepts...106

The Wh - Cycle...106

Convince Yourself..108

Interleaved Practice...110

CHAPTER 7: REINFORCE 112

Embrace Your Mistakes..113

Build Expertise..113

Teach Someone Else...115

CONCLUSION 123

any hardship or damages that may befall them after undertaking information described herein.

Additionally, the information in the following pages is intended only for informational purposes and should thus be thought of as universal. As befitting its nature, it is presented without assurance regarding its prolonged validity or interim quality. Trademarks that are mentioned are done without written consent and can in no way be considered an endorsement from the trademark holder.

Introduction

Congratulations on downloading *Accelerated Learning* and thank you for doing so.

Pick up any book on the subject of Accelerated Learning, and you'll read pretty much the same thing. Choose your learning environment wisely, set up a routine, find tools that will help you to tap into the knowledge quickly, and use emotions to help you to remember. They may also warn you to identify the learning traps that many people fall into and find a way to avoid them entirely.

Most of that advice is just plain old common sense and something that should be relatively easy to do. At least that's what the books will often tell you. It's true; learning should be as easy as 1-2-3. But for the person who has always struggled to learn, these steps could sometimes feel like sugar to a diabetic. They may be common sense to some, but they are too overly simplified to hold any significant value. When these strategies are not executed correctly, they may seem almost impossible to overcome, causing you more harm than good.

The problem with oversimplified advice is just that. For some people, it is not enough to learn the "rules of learning," but you may also need to understand the whys and the hows too. When you take the time to look deeper into how we learn, what it actually means, your eyes begin to open up more channels of learning that you may have previously overlooked.

We've all seen accelerated learners in school. They are the ones that can bury themselves in a book, absorbing every word making even the toughest of subjects seem simple. They are the ones that ace every test with only a few minutes of study, and yet not everyone is not like that. Some people can't learn just from picking up a book, no matter how hard they try. Others need to have more interaction for the information to stick. Even those who are good learners may struggle to keep track with how much they have to learn.

Whatever the case, it is more important than ever that we all speed up our method of learning. We are now deeply involved and settled into the Information Age. Never before in the history of mankind has the amount of intellectual material we need to absorb been so great. Education is no longer the domain for the vibrant minds of our youth but should be of primary concern for parents, educators, business people, and governmental leaders.

This is because things are changing at a never before seen rate. Being able to learn quickly is a must for anyone who wants to succeed in life. Not only do you need to absorb the information faster, but you also need to master the intricate complexities of the material you're learning. Here in this book, you will learn the core skills needed to not only learn faster but to become a more skillful learner.

In the following chapters, we will give you key recommendations on how you can transition from being an occasional learner to a lifelong learner without being overwhelmed by the wealth of information you will have to absorb.

Every day, we see the traditional jobs disappear, being relegated to automated machinery and technology. At the rate that careers are changing, it is only a few decades more, and the only jobs available will be those with finely honed skills and expertise in specific areas. Artificial Intelligence and other forms of modern technology will eventually take over the massive amounts of manpower that are enveloping us now. Soon, jobs that require low-level education will no longer exist. To that end, it is necessary to change our complete view of learning. It is no longer enough for a school to teach us facts and figures; they must also teach us "how to learn." If we don't know how to learn, we will find ourselves firmly stuck between a rock and a hard place, searching desperately for a way to move forward with whatever goals we may have.

Learning is not just about knowing the answers to the questions. It's learning where to look for the answers, learning how to explore, to create, to engage the senses. It's now a matter of continuous analyzation of the world around us. Here, you will learn:

- What it means to learn something
- How to prepare your learning environment
- How the brain and your mind learns
- How memory plays a role and how to kick it in gear
- The six proven steps that lead to faster learning
- Alternative learning approaches
- And how to keep it all active once you get started.

Learning how to learn is not good enough in this modern day and age. You must also learn how to keep learning. Your age, economic status or social position doesn't matter when it comes to learning. Everyone in the twenty-first century needs to be able to keep up with this fast-moving influx of new knowledge, or it will overtake us. To do that, we must continue to learn how to learn, and fast.

If you're ready, get on mark..........get set.......... Let's go!

There are plenty of books on this subject on the market. Thanks again for choosing this one! Every effort was made to ensure it is full of as much useful information as possible, please enjoy!

Chapter 1: This Book is for Whom?

There is no doubt that education and learning have become two of the most important commodities we need in these modern times. We live in a world where communication is instant, where we can talk to people from all walks of life on a daily basis. Even the most mundane of jobs will have us venturing across cultural, economic, and social boundaries that once kept us apart.

The world's data banks are growing at an unprecedented rate. Knowledge, as we know it today, is doubling on the average of every two to three years. Consider some of these facts:

- It takes only four billionths of a second for a computer to process an operation.

- E-mail can traverse the globe on a hair-thin optical fiber in a fraction of a second.

- With satellites, we can have face to face conversations with people all over the world.

- The average American household has access to hundreds of TV channels for their entertainment with a simple click of a button.

- Research projects that at one time would take years to complete can now be completed in a matter of minutes or weeks.

Being able to master new knowledge at a faster rate is no longer favorable but necessary. So, if you are a student trying to gain new knowledge in your field of interest, if you're someone working to gain a competitive edge, if you're looking to advance your career, a professional looking to impress your clients, a parent needing to help your children, or you simply just want to learn more, this book is a must for you.

The reality is that learning is no longer something you do in school. It does not happen during set hours of the day and is not something reserved for those young, nimble minds that can absorb facts, figures, and data faster.

Learning is now a lifelong endeavor. It is now an all-consuming investment in the future. Along with all the modern technology we are enjoying, we have to be able to adapt to new environments and experiences in a blink of an eye.

Part of the reason for this rapid change lies in what's happening in the job market today. In nearly every corporate office in America, there is talk about an increasingly competitive market. Companies are also being pressed to produce faster in order to stay ahead of the competition. For this reason, automating many jobs is not just about improving their bottom line, but it also means they must make these kinds of hard decisions just to keep the doors open.

To do this, companies are making a trade. Where manpower was once their most valuable asset, it is now being replaced by software. Those jobs that did not require deep skills are slowly being replaced by machines. So the number of jobs a person could once get with only minimal education is quickly being depleted. For those who want to keep working, learning how to operate basic machinery is no longer a viable option. Instead, you must put yourself on the other end and learn how to operate the machinery from a vantage point in the cyber world. As an example, look at the list below and see what is happening with many of the jobs many of us have come to rely on.

- In the last decade of the 1900s, more than 1.8 million manufacturing jobs vanished, while productivity in those same companies increased by 35%.

- In the European Union, there were so many people unemployed that if they were all put in a single line, it would reach halfway around the globe.

- Today, only 17% of the world's workforce is in blue-collar manufacturing and only 2% actually still work in agriculture.

- Three to four jobs are lost for every new automated robot brought online. According to *The Financial Times of London*, there will be four times more robotic workers introduced into the business world within the next decade.

- In less than ten years, more than half the textile workers in the United States and in Western Europe were replaced by computerized systems.

- 60% of mine workers and 50% of steelworker jobs have already disappeared, and 30% of the world's tire makers were replaced by automation all within less than a decade.

Over the years, major industry leaders have been forced to make huge changes in how they do business simply because of the rush of new technology being introduced.

Companies that were once well established like General Electric, Kodak, and Xerox have been forced to downsize, letting go hundreds of thousands of employees. It may seem like such drastic measures would ring a death knell to these companies. But the reality is that by switching to automation, many of them have tripled their sales and productivity in the process.

No one knows exactly when or even if this downward spiral is going to come to an end, but there is only one thing we all can be sure of. Those whose jobs will last the longest will be those who are on the opposite end of the spectrum, those who are quick to learn new skills, master new talents, and will be able to change horses in the middle of the stream.

There is no way to predict exactly where this new trend is taking us but we can be assured that as long as we can keep learning new things, we will be in a better position to stake a claim on whatever new industry is coming down the line and we can be the first in line to take advantage of it. So, when the question is asked, who needs to learn faster, the answer should be obvious - All of us.

Chapter 2: Preparing to Learn

To someone who has never planted a garden, the concept is very simple. Dig a hole, plant a seed, cover it up, and put a little water on it. In a very short while you will start to see a shoot break the surface, which will continue to grow until it becomes a full-fledged plant or tree, something that produces fruit, flowers, or foliage for shade.

These are the most fundamental factors to growing any type of plant life, yet they only give an elementary view of what's really involved in gardening. It is only when you have the experience of planting a seed that you realize how much preparatory work is involved before you can even think about digging a hole and planting a seed. Fundamentals like these do not talk about what to do if the soil conditions are not right, what to do if the soil is too sandy, too rocky or too hard. What conditions can choke out your seed and kill it before it breaks the surface. How too much water can drown a plant before it has a chance to get strong.

The basic rules of gardening can also apply to education. Before you can be a successful learner, it is very important that you prepare the soil of your mind so that you can retain much of the knowledge you will be taking in. In order to do this, it is imperative that you lay the right groundwork and set the stage for your learning.

After many years of scientific research and countless studies, we are beginning to get a real grasp on what happens when the brain learns something. It is amazing that it has taken us this long to achieve this point because we have been learning all of our lives. From the moment we take our first breath until we take our last, our brains have been uniquely designed to learn, but we still must lay the proper groundwork for the best results.

One of the first things we must come to understand is that there are many factors, limitations, and conditions that can either enhance or restrict our ability to learn. We need to understand these characteristics before we can begin to accelerate the learning process. Of course, understanding them is only the first step. Some factors that can influence your learning will be easily managed and controlled, but others will create obstacles that could get in the way, and you'll have to devise a means of overcoming them. To put it simply, it is up to you to create the right conditions to optimize your ability to learn. If you don't go into the process with a good plan in place, you may end up sabotaging yourself in the process.

What Exactly is Learning

A huge factor that could be hampering your ability to learn at a faster rate is the confusion surrounding the learning process itself. If you speak to those who lived only a few generations ago, the concept of learning was strictly limited to listening to a person of authority and doing exactly what they said. It did not involve any in-depth thinking process. Schools during those generations primarily produced 'human parrots' where students had no opinions to speak of. They produced generations of people prepared to enter the workforce as factory workers where their primary role was to stomp out an endless array of copies of some product or another. Only a few received the privilege of advancing to higher education or entering fields where specialized knowledge was needed.

Today, the demand for that kind of workforce is steadily dwindling, requiring all of us to use much more brain power than in the past. As a result, the learning process has been extended far into our adult years. Our whole approach to learning also needs to be extended. So, what exactly does it mean to learn within the framework of our modern society? To put it in the simplest of terms, learning is the ability for the mind to absorb and comprehend new information and retain it. It is the acquisition of knowledge in a way that allows us to use it.

In the past, learning was usually a role relegated to schools. But learning can now happen anywhere, at any time, and in any place. Not only can you learn from books, but most likely the most effective and most memorable way of learning is from personal experience.

Most people view learning as an 18-year-long cram session where information is poured into the brain in much the same way as one would stuff a sausage. But the actual meaning of learning is exactly the opposite. Rather than having someone throw a lot of facts and figures at us, we instead need to focus more on extracting information from someone or something. This shifts the responsibility of learning to the student.

You may need to draw out a specific talent or skills that are inherent inside each of us. You may need to pull out old data that you learned years ago, or it just may mean drawing up this new knowledge from an adventure or discovery. To that end, our learning must start within ourselves and expand out, rather than looking outward for what to put in our minds.

How Memory Plays a Role

There is no doubt that the human brain is fascinating too. Its innate ability to grasp concepts, ideas, facts, and more and then frame them in a way that we can use seems deceivingly simple, but in reality, it's a very complex process. What's even more amazing is the brain's ability to file things away; keeping them stored for sometimes years, and then being able to retrieve it when needed.

Yes, your memory is just as important as your ability to learn. It does no one any good to learn all the many aspects and facts of life only to forget them in the future. To become an accelerated learner, it is extremely important that we maintain the ability to reflect on the past and find ways to use it in the present. When we can recall certain events or facts, we are ensuring that there is a certain level of continuity between what has happened and a direct connection to what will be.

How to View Failure

One factor that often gets in the way of learning is our perception of the experiences that we have each day. The general idea that we fail more often than we succeed can be problematic when we attempt to learn new things. There is a saying that "failure is a necessary precursor to ultimate success." This understanding informs an individual that before one can succeed, they must fail, sometimes many times before learning kicks in and you begin to reap the benefits.

However, while this gives us a relatively positive view of failure, others have already been programmed to believe that failure is a result of them being less than what they should be; that their failure is somehow a reflection of their quality as a person. This kind of thinking often comes from the mechanical teaching styles and the rigid grading systems of the last hundred or so years of schooling.

If you don't achieve a set-score by a certain date, then you are deemed unworthy of moving ahead in school. Because you couldn't recall certain facts and dates, you received a poor grade and were told that if you didn't improve, your chances of landing a decent job in the future is practically impossible .

But in the natural scheme of things, it is easy to see that this kind of thinking can be debilitating for many. Failure is a natural part of life. As we learn new things, we will inevitably fail. However, that is no indication that our future success is doomed because of it. As we develop new skills, hone our talents, and embrace new knowledge, we will make mistakes, but these should be viewed merely as a natural part of the journey, not a reflection of who we are at the core.

History is full of people who have failed often but were able to learn from those mistakes and move on. Thomas Edison failed thousands of times before he finally hit upon the secret that led him to invent the first light bulb. And although Michael Jordan had over 9,000 missed shots in his entire career, no one knows him for those misses. They only remember him for the many successful shots he made. Even Oprah Winfrey was fired and deemed "unfit for television" before she made her mark in the TV world.

The bottom line is, it is not the failure that deems you unworthy of success, but it's what you do with it. Throughout everyone's life, there is a long trail of failures. When you first started to walk, you fell many times. When you first realized that you had a talent for something or other, you failed at it many times. Whether speaking, walking, writing, reading, singing, dancing, driving, and so on, no one gets it right every time.

So, rather than view a failure as a blight on your character, which can discourage you from attempting to learn and try again, view it as a mere stepping stone that will eventually lead you to success. The reality is that failure is a common occurrence that we all have in our uncertain world and just a natural part of being human.

As you go through the learning process, you can reasonably expect to fail. When you do, rather than allow them to defeat you, try these steps instead:

1. Reflect: Take the time to go back and look at what went wrong and see if there are ways to avoid repeating it. Was it an error in judgment or were you careless? By reflecting on what happened, you can ensure that you won't repeat the same mistake again in your next attempt.

2. Accept responsibility: Accept responsibility for anything that was within your control. Think about your actions in the situation and decide what you can do differently next time to avoid it. Perhaps you need more training, or you've taken on too much.

3. Refocus: Rather than beat yourself up because you made a mistake, use your energy to refocus on what you can do next. Always look forward rather than dwelling on the past.

4. Plan: Take the time to plan out exactly what steps you will take on your next attempt.

You should also avoid doing the following things:

1. Don't ignore it and move on to something else. Dismissing them as trivial can be just as dangerous as giving them too much attention and allowing them to discourage you.

2. Don't make excuses: Own your mistakes; they are part of your growing process. It is nature's way of giving you a chance to redirect and change course. While there may have been other factors at play (economy, careless coworkers, etc.), accept your role in that failure and move on.

3. Don't hide them: If you attempt to cover them up, you are denying yourself the valuable lessons they can teach you. It can limit how much you can improve.

4. Give up: Failures do not necessarily mean a demise of your goals. Remember that they are part of the natural process of learning. Giving up too soon may feel like you're making a safe move, but you are really

limiting yourself and leaving an opening for someone else to make the success of what you set out to do.

Embrace your failures and use them as one of your most valuable learning tools. By doing so, you will be compelled to move out of your comfort zone and expand your horizons. Of course, this doesn't mean that you should throw all caution to the wind and jump in without any thought to consequences. However, if you're failing even though you have a well-planned program at work, then you are on the right track. Do whatever is in your power to succeed but don't disregard failure or put too much emphasis on it if you don't. Instead, use that experience to learn from and to improve, and you will find that your failures will turn out to be the most memorable part of your learning process, a key factor in how fast you learn, and how strong you will grow.

Knowledge, Understanding, Wisdom: What's the Difference?

We often use the words, knowledge, understanding, and wisdom interchangeably, not realizing the differences that they represent. But there is a real importance in distinguishing the subtle nuances that exist between them. All of them are outstanding qualities that all of us should develop, but our ability to develop them could have a direct impact on how well we accelerate our learning ability. In fact, the more of these differences you can identify, the better your learning process will be.

Knowledge: our main purpose for attending school is to gain knowledge. It is merely the accumulation of facts and figures that relate to the world around us. To put it in its most basic of terms, knowledge is developing an awareness of everything that we interact with within our lives. This knowledge is really the first level of learning in everything we do. Without knowledge, you can never have understanding or wisdom.

Understanding: it is not enough to "know" or to be "aware" of something. Knowledge on its own does not change us or our circumstances. What does change is the carrying of that knowledge forward and recognizing the possible consequences of the decision we make based on that knowledge. Understanding simply means the ability to analyze a situation and recognize the potential results that can be experienced based on the actions and decisions we make using that knowledge.

Wisdom: is the power behind the knowledge you have gained. Once you knew something and understood what options you have and their possible consequences, wisdom comes into play. It is the ability to use that knowledge to make a decision. It is our ability to discern and choose the best path in any given situation.

In most cases, schools focus almost entirely on dispensing knowledge but rarely focus on helping you to develop understanding and wisdom. In order to learn well, it is important that you develop and hone your skills in all three areas. While knowledge can be acquired through reading, listening, observing, and experiencing things; without applying passion and motivation, you would become a receptacle for facts, figures, statistics and such and nothing more.

Without emotion and other internal qualities at work, your knowledge will not amount to much and will not improve your circumstances to any significant degree. This is why you often see young children go to school, cram their minds full of facts, pass the test, and then promptly forget everything they have learned in the process.

To accelerate your learning and grasp things much faster and easier, you will have to apply the other two qualities in order to make the best choices for your life. If you are successful in this, and you repeatedly practice these three elements of learning, then in time, you will develop one of the most valuable qualities you could have. That of insight, a deeper understanding of your world and the choices you have.

All of this can best be described with a simple illustration. Imagine yourself having to walk a long distance. You have two choices before you. First, you could take the long way around and get there safely, or you could take a shortcut and follow the train tracks to your destination in half the time.

Your awareness of the two routes is your knowledge - you understand that both routes will take you to your destination. Recognizing that taking the shortcut following the train tracks would get you there faster but is riskier is your understanding. The decision you make would represent your wisdom.

Of course, other factors will also need to come into play when making these decisions; how urgent is the trip? How much time do you have to make the journey? How important is your value of safety? Do you know the schedule of the trains?

The list can go on, but based on these three qualities, your decision could mean life or death for you. Learning is not just a means of gathering facts and storing them away; it is a full mental exercise where the knowledge you learn must be analyzed and given practical application before it can become of any good and relevant use to you. To do any of that, you must first lay the proper groundwork for effective education by first preparing the mind and the heart to learn.

Preparing the Mind

Up until now, preparing to learn meant accumulating lots of books and reading, reading, and reading. When that was done, your next step was to read some more. However, after decades of scientific studies, a better approach to learning has been identified. The brain (which we will discuss in more detail in the following chapter) is naturally designed to learn.

When you consider that a baby can learn everything he needs to know to survive within the first few years of life, we can see that while reading is a beneficial tool to facilitate learning, it is not, by far, the only one, nor is it the most important one. During most of our lives, our minds are an amazing receptacle for knowledge. In most cases, it is constantly flowing - in at an impressive rate. In fact, your success as a student often relied on how well you could parrot back the information you took in. There was no choice in the matter, and all you had to do was become a good parent to be considered as a good learner.

This often gave many the misleading notion that regurgitation of knowledge was an accurate measure of how well you learned and that it was simply a matter of automation. Like a machine, data was fed into us and the more of it we can spew back – out determined our roles in society.

Today, however, we are learning that there are plenty of other factors (internal and external) that must also be considered before we can learn well. Some are well within our ability to control, and others are not. We are going to now take a closer look at some of these factors and how they can affect our ability to learn. Once you understand them fully, then you will know exactly how to mentally prepare yourself for accelerated learning.

Human attention span:

One of the most important factors to consider is your attention span. All of us have completely different abilities to focus. According to the non-profit organization Technology, Entertainment, and Design, also known as TED Talks, a group focused on sharing ideas from every aspect of our lives through videos, the maximum attention span for the average person is around 18 minutes.

This is an interesting fact that can be of valuable interest to those who are trying to accelerate the learning process. As their curator says, this time frame is just long enough to engage in serious topics but not so long that people will begin to lose their focus. When you look at classes and other types of learning environments, it is clear that this point has been lost on many people. Classes that are running one hour or more are losing the majority of their attendees. By offering them shorter learning sessions, they are better able to absorb the information they are taking in. They can really think about the topic and analyze it carefully so that they can make a more informed decision about what comes next.

Unlike movies, which are passive activities, when the brain is overwhelmed with too much information at one time, it can become fatigued and less productive. If pressed at such an intense schedule for too long, the brain will begin to shut down until it gets a chance to recharge, either by means of a distraction or some form of relaxation.

No matter how much you want to, your mind can only absorb information when it is focused on the topic. Therefore, as Ellen Dunn of Louisiana State University's

Center for Academic Success suggests, learning periods should be limited to sessions between 30 and 50 minutes for the best possible results. This is more important when you are attempting to absorb new material.

Another study that supports the theory of shortening learning periods was done by researchers William Dement and Nathaniel Kleitman as far back as the 1950s. According to their results, the human body usually functions best in 90-minute cycles. They labeled this pattern the "ultradiun rhythm."

Within each of these cycles, there are different segments. The initial segment is the "arousal" period, followed by the mid-period where the highest of performances are met, and lastly, the decelerating period. This period works in the same general vein as the more familiar 24-hour "circadian rhythm," which helps us to see exactly how well we will function throughout the course of a single day.

By making sure your study time is when you are at your mid-period segment of the cycle, you will be mentally capable of absorbing more material in a shorter period of time, facilitating a much faster learning process.

Learning over short bursts of time

All these studies performed over decades have made it clear that the best learning environment needs to be performed in more frequent lessons over shorter periods of time. By allowing our minds to have more time to reset in between sessions, we can literally absorb more information without having to commit to hours of study. To do this, though, it is imperative that you have a good and reliable schedule in order to facilitate this type of learning process.

Start by considering your daily routine. First, determine what times of the day you are the most productive. Some of us may be early morning workers while others may prefer to burn the midnight oil. Block out your learning routine based on the times where you are more productive, and then select several 90-minute sessions that will allow you enough time for breaks in between.

Within each of those 90-minute sessions, the mid-period (where the majority of learning will take place) should be one of those 30-50 minutes of serious study or analysis. This will be the period of time when you are most focused and driven.

As you implement this new schedule, make sure that you are prepared to make the necessary adjustments. No one will be able to get this type of scheduling done right the first time so don't be discouraged if you miss your mark a few times. Review it on a weekly basis and make sure you tweak it wherever you fail to meet your mark. You may have to start with a 30 – minute session and expand it up to 50-minutes if you find it too slow, or you may start with longer sessions and cut back if you find it too long. The goal is to find the right period where your brain is entirely focused and then engaged and maximize that time for your learning.

Surface learning vs. Deep learning

As you set about the learning process, you need to know the difference between surface learning and deep learning. When you are only interested in gaining facts and applying memorization techniques, you are engaged in surface learning. Deep learning, however, is what you are really trying to achieve. This is the practice of analyzing what you are learning so you can extract the underlying meaning and apply it to the real world.

Don't assume that surface learning is not important. In fact, there is a time and a place for both. Some things are best learned through memorization techniques, and other things will require a much deeper form of study in order to grasp the full impact of it. Suffice to say, if you are going to apply deep learning methods to your study, it is very important that you make sure that you do it during your peak attention span so you can absorb more of it.

A general rule of thumb to follow when studying is to first grasp the concepts of a topic. Once the concepts are understood, you can then reach for the facts, which are more surface learning styles. Then make sure you fully understand the context of the material before you try to commit them to memory.

Concepts before Facts, Understanding before Memory

You also want to make a point to look for patterns. Nearly everything you learn will have some type of pattern to help you relate to it. It is the patterns that help you to see concepts and connections between what you are learning and how you can use it. Without them, what you are learning won't have much value to you. It is also these patterns that will help the brain absorb the data and remember it later when you need it. In fact, it is more likely that you will recall the pattern before you recall the fundamentals of any lesson you take on.

To understand how this works, think of the details surrounding a single historical event. Let's say, we want to understand how the abolition of slavery came about. Yes, you could learn the date of the Emancipation Proclamation, you could learn all the facts of the Civil War, Abraham Lincoln, the state of the political government at the time, or you might even learn a little bit about the life of a slave during those tumultuous years.

However, those are just simple facts that do not have any significant relevance to you in this present day and age. Those facts won't give you much incentive to recall them to mind. However, if your focus is on the larger concept of the abolition of slavery, how it changed the course of history, how it started an entire revolutionary movement, that it was impetus that eventually leads to the Civil Rights Movement, how it impacted the lives of everyone in the nation whether they owned slaves or not, how it has a direct impact on how people view you even today, then the power of the lesson will ring true. By making those connections, you now have more of an incentive to focus on the facts and have a much better chance of remembering them.

This is referred to as concept learning. The ability to categorize what you are learning based on certain elements. It's like tying a string to the pattern and following it right back to your mind and heart. If your mind has been properly prepared, then you are more likely to not only grasp the fundamentals of what you are learning but also be able to recall it when needed.

Preparing the Heart

We've already discussed how important emotion is to the learning process. It's a key element that is very instrumental in enhancing the memory process. To engage the heart means to have some motivation that drives you to want to learn. If you've ever been a classroom teacher, then you understand exactly how difficult it is to get a student who is unmotivated to apply him or herself.

It's literally impossible to get them to study, to read, or to take even the slightest interest in the subject matter. To engage the heart means that you have to discover the reason why you need to learn these things.

Think of this phase like reading a recipe for a dish. You might want to prepare your favorite sauce for a dinner. You look in a cookbook, choose a recipe and follow the steps exactly. If you've done so carefully and correctly, the result will be a beautiful sauce that you can proudly serve to your family.

If you follow this recipe enough times, chances are after a time, you won't need the recipe anymore. You will have memorized all of the steps. However, you won't be able to expand on that knowledge and apply it to other meals you might make. Unless you know exactly why you need to sweat the onions, you won't understand how that same technique can be used in other dishes. If you don't know why it is necessary to boil the sauce first and then let it simmer, then you won't understand the reason why the flavors blend so well together.

The more you understand "your why," the more motivated you'll be to take in the information. Your mind will be more open and receptive to what you're learning and will give it more attention.

Another way you can engage the heart is to connect to a positive experience in the past. There may be times when you may need to learn something, and you just can't seem to get yourself motivated. There is no inner drive that will compel you to want to learn. When that happens, you can trick your mind and heart into cooperating. Try this exercise when situations like that begin to happen.

For this, you will have to use a personal memory to help you. Think back to a pleasant and happy experience in your life. Ideally, you want to choose something that made you really excited about a past success. Once you've formed it in your mind, try to remember how it made you feel. Think about what was happening around you. Were people congratulating you, was there lots of praise, did people smile, hug, kiss, or compliment you? The more details you can recall about the event, the better.

Relish at that moment for a while. This technique is called "triggering." When you're in that state of mind, you'll be in the best mental, emotional, and spiritual state for learning. Doing this exercise before engaging in a humdrum lesson that is dull and uninspiring could literally move you to want to try harder and take more interest in what you are about to study. This exercise brings together not just emotions but also blends your feelings and memories together in the same place, like a perfect pasta sauce.

Preparing the Environment

When it comes to making your environment conducive to learning, most people think of setting up a quiet place without distractions. While that is important, it is not the only focus for learning that you can use. You also want to try to create your own mental cocoon; something that will separate you from the external chaos around you.

This means finding a place where you feel comfortable enough to kick back and relax. Get into a comfortable position. For some people, this means taking off their shoes, listening to some pleasant music (make it soothing, the harsher the music, the more invasive it will be on the brain) something soft to allow effective studying.

Now, set up your study space with things that make you feel relaxed and comfortable. This could be anything from pleasing artwork to plants. Make sure you have a strong infusion of fresh, clean, air - or better yet, find a place outside where you can study in a more natural environment.

It is not enough to have a place of solitude. Your environment must be conducive to an open - frame of mind. Having a place where you naturally feel relaxed and at peace can help bring your mental and emotional state into harmony so you can focus on what you're about to study.

Chapter 3: Your Learning Arsenal

Learning is a complex process, and it is not as easy as just listening to what someone tells you and remembering it. In order for you to become a truly efficient learner, you need to understand a great deal about yourself and what is involved in the learning process. As with any other tool you might use, there is one single tool that is most important over all others.

Our brain has been studied for centuries by the best biologists, psychologists, scientists, educators, and many others. And what's their goal? To give a complete description of the brain and explain how it works. Still, even today, they are just beginning to get a clear picture of what happens in the brain when we learn. Once you understand the complex mechanisms involved, you'll be able to see clearly how best to feed your mind with information so that you can learn.

The Brain - How does it Work?

Interestingly enough, the brain is a highly functioning organ that comes in a hundred billion pieces all working together. While that number sounds impressive, the way the brain works doesn't depend entirely on the number of brain cells (neurons) you have but on the number of "connections" (synapses) that exist between those cells. Each one of those neurons has the ability to grow as many as 20,000 branches or dendrites. This means that the total number of connections may not actually be countable but even without knowing the exact number of these connections, we can be confident that the human brain is capable of absorbing much more than what we are currently learning now.

Because of all the studies that have been conducted, we are now able to "see" exactly how a thought, memory, fear, or emotion enters into the brain's conscious mind. We can now understand better what exactly happens when we learn.

As a result, we have learned one extremely important factor that is essential to the learning process. For the brain to be at its optimum learning condition, it must be exercised regularly. Without regular use, the brain will weaken and become ineffective. So, let's take a look at what happens in the brain when you learn and how you can exercise it regularly so that you can get it to its optimum level of performance.

We've all seen pictures of the human brain. The folded layers of what appears to be fatty tissue all intertwined together seem almost alien in nature. In actuality, you're not looking at just one brain, but you have three brains working for you. While it may sound like something out of a science fiction movie, *The Man with Three Brains,* at its core, it is really very basic in nature.

The Reptilian Brain

Sometimes referred to as the brain stem, the reptilian brain is the most primal of all. It is the one common feature that we share with other lower life forms including reptiles (hence the name the reptilian brain) and birds. This is the part of the brain that controls your body's basic functions; those things we do without any kind of thought or planning; breathing, keeping our heart beating, and our instinctive responses (fight or flight).

This is the part of the brain that also controls our sense of personal space, territory, and emotions. This is one of the reasons why knee-jerk emotions like anger are difficult to control. When you sense a threat or perceive someone trying to invade your space or your territory, the response you give is instinctive in nature.

The Mammalian Brain

More properly known as the limbic system, the mammalian brain is the central part of the brain that wraps itself around the brain stem. This part of the brain is very similar to the brains of any other mammal. Inside the limbic system are two key components, the hypothalamus, and the amygdala. This is the part of the brain that controls all of your emotions. It is also responsible for keeping the body stable and running smoothly.

Here is where you produce hormones and have your natural urges stimulated. Thirst, hunger, and sex urges are all stimulated in the pleasure center, which is part of the limbic system. It is also the part of the brain that manages your body's immune system, your metabolism, and the most important element, your long-term memory.

All of these functions are managed by the hypothalamus and the amygdala, which is the seat of your emotional behavior and your desire to achieve your goals. This is one reason why people are more inclined to respond to an emotional appeal rather than a rational argument.

It is important to recognize that the same part of the brain that is responsible for controlling your emotions also controls your long-term memory. This is a key factor in understanding how you learn. If you have an emotional experience, it will be remembered much quicker than one that you are not emotionally invested in.

Think back to big events in your past. What were you doing on 9/11, when Hurricane Katrina hit, or the tsunami that struck Southeast Asia? No doubt, you can remember exactly where you were when you first heard the news. So, the more emotion you get out of a learning experience, the more able you'll be to remember it. This effect is much more effective if you're using a positive experience rather than a negative one. Simply by adding on the positive emotions to the learning process, will add an even more powerful emotional level that will help you retain what you are learning.

You can do this by adding in elements of the lesson that can inspire your passion. Rather than have all of your studies done in black and white, consider adding things like art, music, drama, color, emotion, and even games to help speed up the process.

While you can learn to a certain degree when negative emotions are involved, researchers Mortimer Mishkin and Tim Appenzeller suggested in an article for Scientific American, that you may learn from the experience but may not always have that information readily available when called up later. Negative emotions actually trigger the brain to downshift to the reptilian brain, which operates more often by instinct rather than any other element. The bottom line is, stress can actually inhibit the learning process so your focus should be to keep your emotional and mental state as positive and upbeat as possible.

The Thinking Brain

The more advanced part of the brain is the Thinking Brain or the Neocortex. This wraps over the other two types of brains. This part of the brain, if spread out on a table in front of you, is probably be the same size of a newspaper page.

The Thinking Brain is truly unique and is at the heart of all things considered intelligent. It is actually the part of the brain that makes us stand out as "human." From the neocortex, we are able to receive data from our five senses. We develop our creative mind, and we use our reasoning abilities. This is the part of the brain that makes decisions, organizes our lives, and produces speech.

So, we can see things in an abstract manner like with paintings and in a dance. We can get enjoyment from music, and other less defined types of knowledge. The neocortex is where the heart of the learning happens.

This part of the brain is divided into two lobes that handle all of our speech, hearing, vision, and touch. The strongest memories we store are those that engage all of the senses. So, if you hear it, say it, see it, and do it, all at the same time, you will definitely remember it.

In our prefrontal lobes, located right behind the forehead, you learn how to exercise judgment, plan for your future, and develop a higher order of thinking. This area of the brain has a direct link to your limbic system where you show your compassion and sense of what is right and wrong.

All of these parts of the brain work together to make humans distinctive from every other creature on earth. It is the reason why our ability to think is so much more advanced than other animals. This is where we get the ability to adapt to a world with constantly changing circumstances.

The Two Minds

While the three parts of our brain all work together to give us all of these capabilities, the brain's functions go much further. When you look at the brain in its entirety, you will notice that it can be divided into two hemispheres, which you've probably heard being referred to as the left and the right brain.

While we have known for thousands of years that the left brain controlled sensations from the right side of our bodies and the right from the left side, it's only been in the last few decades that we've really begun to understand the two hemispheres and what they actually do.

We now know that both hemispheres are designed to do very different things. While they are both connected by an impressive array of hundreds of millions of neurons, information is sent back and forth between the two halves at an incredible speed giving each side something unique to do.

The left brain functions more in the academic arena and processes our language, mathematics, reasoning, and analysis whereas the right brain is the more creative side. It is where our artistic abilities reside; music, art, and conceptual thought. This is also the area that deals with intangible concepts of life including love, appreciation for beauty, and loyalty.

While you might think that these are two completely separate aspects of our thought process, our brains are far too complex to simply relegate these concepts to a single area. Even though they may be the center of their areas of thought, because of the trillions of synapses that are constantly firing, communication between each of these areas is constantly happening. While one hemisphere may be dominant in processing a certain bit of knowledge, they are both participating in the process to some degree.

It is, however, the method of processing information that you need to be concerned with when trying to speed – up your learning. If you are a person with a predominant left brain, then you would most likely want to obtain your information in a methodical, step-by-step manner. This is referred to as linear learning. Those with a predominant right brain, tend to want to approach the subject by getting overview of the topic; its global perspective.

Ask yourself, when you listen to a song, what does your mind focus on? Right brain people will be more in tune to the melody and the music while left-brain people will focus more on the lyrics. Even so, your whole brain will be participating in the absorption of that information. Because music has elements that are strong both in the right and left hemispheres, it is much easier for people to learn through music, especially when the lyrics are delivered with deep feeling and emotion.

Intelligence - What is it, really?

For generations, our intelligence has been measured by a test created by a French psychologist named Alfred Binet. The test was devised as a means of identifying those students that had some form of learning disability. Most of us are familiar with an IQ test and can even recite our score if asked. However, beginning in the twentieth century's last decades, many people started to question this type of test's accuracy.

The IQ or the Intelligence Quotient was determined by dividing the mental age over the chronological age of an individual then multiplying the answer to 100. While there is no question that an IQ test can accurately measure a student's potential in an academic setting, it has not proven to be an accurate assessment of an individual's overall intelligence.

Look at any IQ test, and you'll see why there are definitely some loopholes that will cause many to fall through the cracks. The test focuses almost entirely on left brain concepts: areas of language, mathematics, and spatial tasks. So, for anyone with a predominant right brain, their ability to score well on such a test could be severely hampered.

Ideas began to change with the introduction of a new definition of intelligence provided by Harvard Professor, Howard Gardner. He asked the proverbial question; how would an alien from another world measure our intelligence. Would he 1) ask for each person's IQ or 2) would he gauge it by observing humans performing within their own environment, those who excel like chess masters, an orchestra conductor or even a musician or an athlete?

He questioned why those with extremely high IQs often ended up working for those with relatively average IQs. As a result, he came up with what we now know as the Theory of Multiple Intelligences. His belief was that our intelligence should not be measured in the same way we would measure our height, weight, or blood pressure. It is not a fixed entity that can be understood and measured by a simple test. The conclusion is, *"It's not how smart you are but how you are smart."*

Every human being has his own battery of skills where he is stronger in some areas than in others. When necessary, he calls on these skills to solve problems. This battery of skills is the person's own unique form of intelligence; which can be defined as the *"ability to solve a problem or fashion a product that is valued in one or more cultural settings."*

So, your intelligence can adapt based on your individual circumstances. In other words, you would need a different type of intelligence if you were lost at sea than the type you would need to navigate the streets of New York City.

Multiple Intelligences

Gardner's theory, which caught on quickly, came from a composite of knowledge gained from studies in the fields of neurobiology, psychology, anthropology, philosophy, and even history. Through these studies, he derived at least eight different types of intelligence.

Linguistic: Those who prefer to learn through reading, writing, and verbal communication. Those who are strong in linguistic intelligence tend to be authors, journalists, comedians, poets, and those in the public speaking arena.

Logical/Mathematical: Those who prefer to learn by reasoning or by performing calculations. These people like to think things through in a very systematic manner. They usually end up as engineers, economists, detectives, accountants, and lawyers.

Visual/Spatial: These are people who have strong visualization skills. They can think about something and see an image of it in the future. They have powerful imaginations and can visualize possibilities. They are often found as architects, artists, photographers, and planners.

Musical: Those who have the ability to create music, to sing well, and have an appreciation for the many nuances found in music. They can keep rhythm, and have some level of talent. Nearly all of us have some level of musical intelligence in us. When you learn anything put to music, it is much easier to remember.

Kinesthetic: Those who have an ability to use their body to find solutions, or to create using physical effort. They are often inclined to present their ideas and emotions in a very physical way. You're more likely to see them as athletes, dancers, actors, or in building and construction occupations.

Interpersonal: These are highly social people that are able to work very effectively with other people. They are capable of displaying empathy and understanding and recognize others' motivations and goals. They are well suited for careers as teachers, therapists, religious leaders, and salespeople.

Intrapersonal: People who are interpersonal have a strong ability to reflect on things, to self-analyze, and contemplate behaviors, inner feelings, and accomplishments. They know how to make plans, establish goals, and can connect with their inner self. They usually make good philosophers and counselors.

Naturalist: Those who can identify flora and fauna in the natural environment and be able to use this knowledge productively. They may be hunters, farmers, or scientists. Many have found careers as biologists, environmentalists, or conservationists.

In the latter part of the twentieth century, Gardner added a ninth intelligence: existential. These people have qualities that authenticate or connect with a higher being. It is often demonstrated in areas where wisdom, compassion, and integrity are necessary. Their personalities usually show qualities of integrity, joy, love, creativity, and peace. They seek for a deeper meaning and purpose in life and usually hold careers in counseling, religion, and leadership.

As we each explore our own battery of intelligence, we'll learn which ones are more dominant in us. While we all have some degree of each of these intelligence, those that we find dominant personally are the ones that will make learning easier and faster for each of us.

Traditionally, academic lessons are geared towards linguistic and logical intelligences so those who are strong in these intelligences will fare much better in traditional learning environments. However, those that are allowed to tap into other intelligences will be better equipped to apply the full might of their brain power to learning.

The beauty of this knowledge is that once you find a way to marshal all of your intelligences together and apply them to learning, there could be no stopping you from what you will be able to learn. You will find that learning is much easier and more fun.

Brain Waves

Your brain is the most complex tool you'll ever use in the learning process. It is a machine that is constantly working, transmitting information on a number of different frequencies much like a radio or television. It is receiving and sending signals simultaneously every day, 24/7.

This is done by means of tiny electrical impulses that cross the brain as thoughts. Think of it, every time you have a thought it is triggered by a small electrical charge shooting through your brain. These electrical impulses can actually be observed and measured by an electroencephalograph machine or an EEG.

Electrodes are first connected to the scalp, and the machine picks them up via brain waves and records the number of cycles per second. There are four different types of brain waves that can be used to carry these impulses. Which one is active at any point in time can vary based on a number of circumstances regardless whether you are awake or asleep. They are Beta, Alpha, Theta, Delta, and Gamma.

Beta: This is the brainwave that is active with your conscious mind. It operates at a rate of thirteen to twenty-five cycles every second, when you are awake, fully attentive, and alert. When the Beta waves are active, your mind is busy analyzing situations, talking, and thinking through problems and situations.

Alpha: Alpha waves occur when the mind is in a relaxed or meditative state. Its cycles are slower, operating at between eight and twelve cycles per second. This is the state of mind when you are daydreaming or imagining. While your mind is relaxed, you are mentally alert at the same time.

Theta: Theta waves appear when you are in the very early stages of sleep. It has a very slow cycle operating at four to seven cycles per second. You could consider this to be the "twilight" of sleep. The mind is sifting through and processing all the data taken in throughout the day. It is the point when you may have many inspirational thoughts.

Delta: Delta waves occur while you're in a deep but dreamless sleep state. It is the slowest, registering only one-half to three cycles per second.

Gamma: There is one more brainwave pattern that is attracting the interest of neurological researchers, and that is the gamma brain waves. It operates at frequencies as high as 40 Hz and has been observed to occur during lucid sleep.

One study completed in 2009 revealed that the gamma state of mind allows a person to be dreaming but experiencing a wake-like state at the same time or a person who is in what is believed to be a higher state of consciousness; a blend of REM and waking cognition both occurring at the same time.

This knowledge gives us a vital key to our learning process. Knowing which brain waves are most effective for learning can help you tap into your right mental state and choose the best time to buckle down and study. Which time you choose will depend on several different factors. If you're going to be studying complex scientific data, you will want to tackle it during the beta wave cycles. Once you've studied that information, you will need to be in the more relaxed state of alertness of the alpha waves in order to process it.

When in the beta state, you concentrate on absorbing complex information, but the alpha state is when you're in a more relaxed state of mind and are more prone to intuitive thinking. When alpha and theta states are the dominant brain waves, left brain activity becomes stronger. This will normally work as a means of censoring what enters the subconscious mind, making it possible for you to be more emotional and creative.

When you are ready to learn, your objectives should be to:

- Engage the emotional brain so that you will remember more of what you absorb
- Get both the left and right brain working together

- Try to access all of the eight intelligences so that the learning process is simplified

- Incorporate relaxation periods where the mind can consolidate the information, allowing for better understanding and you will absorb more information in a much shorter period of time.

By utilizing the entire brain, the potential for learning and your ability to remember what you take in will be enhanced.

This is a lot of information to take in. The diagram below can help you to keep it all straight in your head. The brain is the most powerful tool for facilitating learning; the better you understand how it works, the easier it will be to choose the right time for learning to take place and the right methods that will improve how fast you grasp new concepts.

Chapter 4: Your Memory

We've already talked a great deal about memory and the brain, but we've only just begun to scratch the surface of how your memory actually works. Even the act of recalling the simplest of details involves the stimulation of complex neural networks throughout the brain.

Interestingly enough, our memory is not some static function that happens inside the brain but is an active process that is never-ending. It is important to understand that memory is a necessary element of the learning process, but it is not the same. There are actually three important components to memory that you should understand.

- Encoding: the process the brain uses to change data learned into a form that can be held in the memory.

- Storage: the brain's ability to hold the data.

- Retrieval: the brain's ability to re-access the learned data from whatever region it has been stored in.

We'll begin by knowing first the encoding process. Your ability to learn something depends heavily on encoding. When you learn, the brain goes through a selective process that categorizes information into several different areas. First, it looks at the data to see if it is related to the type of material that has already been encoded. In this regard, the content of the data could include quantity of information (the more data you have, the more complex the encoding process can be), how the information is organized, and how familiar you might already be with the information.

All of these factors and more are processed through the brain at phenomenal speeds. In fact, it happens so quickly, you aren't even aware that your brain has done it.

When it comes to encoding, environmental factors also play a role. While they are not always considered to be important, this does factor into how well you remember things. Think back on how unreliable your memory was when the temperature was extremely high, or there was a lot of distracting noise in your environment. While each person is different, these environmental factors could be a very important element that could either inhibit or stimulate your memory and how well you learn.

Other factors that could also affect the encoding process of your memory could be your physical condition. Factors such as fatigue, health, and motivation can contribute significantly to how much of the information is actually imprinted in the brain. This is why you see so many courses that address the issue of "What's in it for me?" as part of their training programs. If you do not have proper motivation, your chances of recalling the data later on will be drastically reduced.

The second phase of memory is storage. Your brain analyzes the information it receives to determine if it is related to certain conditions under which it can be encoded. Once the information is encoded, it must be stored in the brain. If it cannot be stored, no matter what you learn, it will be of no demonstrable use to you.

Our brains' memory storage has two primary types: short - or long-term memory. Both will act as filters that are put in place to ensure and protect the brain from an information overload. We are not aware of just how much data our brain picks up every day. Most of it is naturally disregarded and sifted out so that it doesn't all go into the memory banks.

Information that is considered important is retained while information that is not relevant or does not carry a significant amount of weight is tossed. For example, information that is repeated regularly will be viewed as important and will go into our memory banks but the chill you felt when the wind blew your hat off your head last winter won't. The brain sees it as having no significant relevance to the learning process so it will not be stored (unless you view it as a memorable experience related to something else). The more experience or a piece of data is repeated, the more likely the knowledge will end up in your long-term memory banks.

Finally, there is the process of retrieval or the ability to re-access the stored information, recalling it to mind again. There are many different types of retrieval. Recognition is when the mind associates an event or an object with previous experience. You can recognize a face, the answers to questions on a test, or the sound of a particular song. Recall, on the other hand, involves remembering a specific fact, or a set event, or object. You might recognize a face, but you will recall the name.

The Forgetting Curve

It is important that when you consider memory, you also factor in your forgetting curve. The two actually work together. Whatever your brain chooses not to remember, you will forget. Therefore, it becomes necessary for you to understand that forgetting also changes as you age. After many studies carried out over several years, there has been only one sure fire way to prevent forgetfulness, and that is through repetition, but we'll discuss more of this later in this book.

Suffice to say, without memory your ability to learn is rendered moot. You can't have one without the other. Your memory is the single element that makes it possible for you to link your new knowledge to past experiences. As you start working on your Accelerated Learning Program, it is extremely essential to protect this relationship between learning and memory so you can have the most efficient learning process.

Memory Retention

Because details of a particular event are not stored in exactly the same place in the brain, recalling them requires many parts to work together to assemble previously acquired knowledge. To make this happen there is a tiny little part of the brain that has to be functioning properly - the hippocampus. This straddles both hemispheres and is responsible for collecting new information, sorting it out and turning that information into a real memory before sending it to other areas of the brain to be stored. Without this tool, learning would be possible but memory would not.

In essence, it not only makes it possible to remember, but it also works as an all-important filter in deciding what data is important to remember or what can be discarded, a critical element in the learning process. But all memory is not the same. We've already discussed short-term and long-term memory, but there is a lot more to memory that you must keep in mind.

Five Types of Memory

Neurologist Dr. Murray Grossman and his team at the University of Pennsylvania Medical Center developed an acronym that will allow us to recall the five different types of memory: W-I-R-E-S.

W-Working
I-Implicit
R-Remote
E-Episodic
S-Semantic

By using this acronym, it helps to remember the brain as a device that has been specifically wired to perform certain functions. Let's look at each of these one at a time.

Working: Our working memory is extremely short-term. It lasts for only a few seconds. It's located right in the prefrontal cortex (behind the forehead) and allows you to retain several things in your mind for a limited period of time. This is why you can recall the first words someone has said to you and hold it until you can gather their main thoughts and put them together. With this type of memory, you are also able to multi-tasks - performing several small tasks at the same time. You can have a conversation with one person and wave to someone else and even read simultaneously.

Implicit: Your implicit memory allows you to recall skills you've learned like riding a bicycle, driving, or even swimming. This is why you can learn to ride a bike when you are six and still know how to do it when you are fifty. In layman's terms, we often refer to this as muscle memory. This is also the reason why when you're driving your car, you don't have to concentrate and can lose yourself in thought on other topics and never have to worry about running through a red light or missing your turn. This type of memory is stored in the cerebellum of the brain.

Remote: Our remote memory is the biggest memory storage you can have. It holds all the data you have accumulated and stored throughout your lifetime in your cerebral cortex. It can hold massive amounts of information on a wide variety of topics and never get full. However, older people tend to have trouble during the retrieval phase as they try to access this storage facility, so they must work that much harder to get through such a large store of knowledge.

Episodic: Episodic memory is the recollection of very specific personal experiences. Of course, not all knowledge is stored here but those experiences that you definitely have a connection to: a scene from your favorite movie, the exact location where you parked your car and the result of that Super Bowl game you saw. It stores memories of experiences that gave you a significant level of emotional fulfillment.

Semantic: This type of memory focuses on words and symbols and is the one area that is never forgotten. Words and symbols that are clearly unforgettable can include religious icons, certain expressions, and the fundamentals of how the world works. For example, you may forget everything else, but you will remember what a dog or a cat looks like, the smell of bacon, or your favorite food. It is this type of memory that gives us the foundation on how the world works.

When learning new information, the best way to ensure that you will remember it is to make sure that the lesson has a powerful emotional impact. This includes incorporating the five senses in the learning process and associating it with positive emotions.

New studies are now showing that lessons can be learned, but it is not sealed into your memory banks until you are in a deeply relaxed state or asleep. So, you may be in the beta or alpha stage when you learn but to seal it in your memory your brain must be in the theta brainwave state.

There have been many studies performed on humans and other animals showing that sleep has a powerful ability to boost memory, especially during the rapid eye movement (REM) stage. Repeatedly, studies have shown that during the day the brain is flooded with all sorts of input coming through the five senses, but it is unable to absorb it all while the brain is in this receiving mode. During the REM stage, the receiving mode shuts down giving the brain time to process the events it has taken in. It is during this stage that the brain can sift through everything that make sense of it and file it away in the proper memory file.

This is the primary way we dream, our mind begins to create its own story as the brain attempts to put all the pieces together and make sense of them. Therefore, to facilitate and speed up the learning process, creating easy to visualize stories related to the lesson is a very effective tool that will help you to remember.

This is why expressions like *My Very Energetic Mother Just Served us Nine Pizzas* have been so effective in helping us to recall the planets in the solar system. You can use this technique to help you recall new vocabulary and foreign languages with plenty of visual and auditory aids.

How Emotions Play a Role

Emotion is a powerful force that when used correctly can be very effective in helping you learn. After years of research, we are just beginning to grasp how malleable our mind is when emotions are involved.

It is important, however, to understand that not all emotions are conducive to learning. When associated with negative events, the brain automatically begins to shift to the fight-or-flight response, which begins to flood our system with stress hormones. The brain then uses these chemicals to control how strong the memory storage will be.

These stress hormones make it possible for you to perform certain physical reactions in an attempt to protect yourself. It also will embed into your brain extremely vivid images that you will never forget. Think about the time you were bitten by a dog, your brain will never let you forget that experience, and every time you see a dog after that, those images will come back up triggering the same fight or flight response.

The fact is that it is literally impossible for anyone to separate emotion from the learning process. This is because of all the neural connections in the brain, the majority of them coming from or going to the limbic brain (the emotional center) of the cortex. This makes emotion a more powerful tool for learning than logic.

Although the limbic brain works in much the same way as a switchboard sending all incoming data to the thinking cortex, there is a much faster way for knowledge to get embedded and that is through emotion. Since this kind of information that we have an emotional connection to could be a warning of something that is potentially life-threatening, it does not stop to be analyzed but instead heads directly to the more primal regions of the brain, giving you a more "gut" and instinct reaction.

These areas of the brain rely more on knee-jerk reactions rather than a stage of mental processing. This is why, when you get a slight glimpse of a snake in your path, your mind doesn't go through all the knowledge you have about snakes, but it focuses on how to get away fast without getting harmed.

Use It or Lose It

For older people, memory becomes a tricky thing. While learning is still possible, many think that they are already too old to learn anything new. For many, it is the time when memory begins to fail, and they stop trying.

If you were to follow the statistics, you would think that this is true. After the age of sixty, reported cases of dementia double every five years and after the age of eighty-five, 30 or 40 percent of people will have been affected by some form of memory altering ailment.

However, after many years of study, the decline in one's memory is no longer a foregone conclusion for those of advanced years. According to one study, 25-33% of participants in their eighties scored just as high as the younger ones. Some of them had scores high enough to rank at the top of mental abilities for those of all ages.

What they have learned after such studies is that the previous theory that we begin to lose 100,000 neurons every year is not entirely true. Instead, our brain cells begin to shrink in size or become dormant as we get older, especially if we do not keep them actively engaged. According to researchers at Stanford and the Albert Einstein College of Medicine, the brain does not lose cells but still has the ability to grow new dendrites even in advanced years. The new cell growth is encouraged by stimulation, so as long as you continue to learn, the brain will continue to develop regardless of the age.

Photographic Memory

You might now be wondering about those people who have what is called a photographic memory or eidetic memory. First, let's make it clear what it really is. The general belief is that once a person sees something that memory remains with them. They will be able to readily recall it exactly as it was first seen without fail.

This, however, is a misnomer. Actually, a photographic memory can at times be as faulty as a regular memory. Many factors can have an impact on what they are able to recall; how long they observed the object or event, whether they were consciously trying to study it, or just saw it in passing.

An eidetic memory is simply someone who can observe something in such a way that it leaves a lasting impression that is so strong that the visual image remains firm in the mind's eye even after it is no longer within physical view. In essence, the person remembers it exactly as it has been seen. However, that is only if they imprinted on the image in the first place.

Just because some people can remember details better than others doesn't mean that they have a photographic memory. They have simply developed good learning skills, concentration, and making relevant connections of what may appear to be unrelated data. They may also have a better grasp on how to use mnemonic devices to help facilitate the learning process than other casual observers.

The questions then become, can you develop your own photographic memory? Those who are truly eidetic are rare and are usually born with this innate ability, so they already have a head start. As they mature, they develop it further. There are several internet sites that claim that they can teach you how to develop this skill, but they are basically only offering you general memory improvement strategies. While you can improve your ability to remember things, learning how to develop your own photographic memory will take many years of practice in applying highly effective memory techniques.

Chapter 5: Six Steps to Faster Learning

Learning is a natural process. It starts from the first moment after birth and continues until your last day. Children are natural born learners and inquisitive about everything in their environment. They are little miniature scientists that love to experiment. Since they have yet to learn the arts of reading and writing, everything they learn comes from observation and experimentation.

They don't know that failure is supposed to be bad. If they make a mistake, they do not become distressed and discouraged. Instead, they pick themselves up, and they try again. And they enjoy every aspect of the process as they do. However, at some point, they begin to lose their enjoyment of the learning process. And for some reason, it becomes more of a chore than a pleasurable way to spend their time. This usually starts to happen when stresses are added to the learning process. They have to learn this much data so they can pass a test, they have to maintain a certain GPA, or they won't graduate. The learning environment goes from experimental to a clinical subject by subject approach to knowledge.

If adults could learn to mimic the way a child learns, where pleasure remains the primary focus to acquiring the knowledge, then we will naturally absorb more data and retain it better. If adults were to remember to engage all of the five senses in their lessons, if we can practice all of these things along with our knowledge of how the brain works, then we'd have a powerful recipe for accelerated learning.

This is the theory of psychologist Mihaly Csikszentmihalyi, who has studied the way children learn for more than twenty years. It's a method whereby a person's state of consciousness is so focused on the topic that they are completely absorbed in the activity. It's taking that childlike inquisitiveness and applying it to an adult world.

In order to do this, we have to start to change our mindset. For example, one reason children tend to be such excellent learners is that they have yet to develop certain beliefs about how they are supposed to be learning. They experiment at will without any preconceived ideas about how they should be acquiring their knowledge. They also have yet to be told that play and learning is exclusive of each other. To a child, play is the work, and the work is learning. Therefore, it becomes a highly enjoyable experience, free of stress and obligation.

So, how do we create that kind of learning in the adult world? We need to follow a few basic guidelines to bring out the inner child.

- Create a low-stress environment where there is no judgment, and you are free to make mistakes.
- Make it easy to succeed.
- Make sure the subject is relevant - know your why.
- Make sure that it is emotionally stimulating and positive.
- Add humor and encouragement.
- Take regular breaks.
- Engage all the senses.
- Use both left and right brain hemispheres.
- Apply as many of the intelligences as possible.
- Have a consolidation period afterward where you can relax and review the new knowledge.

There are six steps that make it possible for you to apply these basic guidelines to your accelerated learning program that can be best remembered with the acronym **M-A-S-T-E-R**

Step 1: Motivating the Mind

In the first phase of the accelerated learning plan, you need to get in the right mental state for learning. That doesn't mean cramming lots of data into your head for endless hours of study. To the contrary, you will need to be in a more relaxed frame of mind, confident, and with motivation as your driving force.

Getting in the Right Frame of Mind

The right mental attitude is essential if you want to learn quickly. Accelerated learning leaves you no time for self-doubt or stress, which will only eat up the time you have set aside for proper study. First and foremost, if you **want** to learn, to develop the new skill, or to master new knowledge, you must be confident enough to **believe** that you are capable of mastering your target subject.

To get into a relaxed mental state, start by practicing a few breathing exercises and making a conscious effort to relax your muscles, especially those in your neck and jaw (this is the area where our bodies tend to hold the most tension.)

Then try some visualization exercises which will help to cement the positive image into your mind.

- See yourself applying the knowledge.
- Imagine how you will feel once you've mastered your topic.
- Hear the voices of people as they praise your newfound abilities.

WII-FM (What's In It for Me)

You also need to be able to mentally picture how this information is going to benefit you. It is one of the core ways to motivate you. If you don't believe that you will gain any advantage by having this knowledge, that you won't see any personal benefit to it, you won't be able to generate that driving force to work for it. You must have your own personal reasons for learning. Start by making a list of the reasons why you need this new information, ask yourself questions, and find your whys. As soon as you discover what's in it for you, you will feel that spirit of motivation push you to want to learn, and your mind will open up to receive new knowledge.

Record Successes

Now, you want to recall some feel-good moments from your past. Think of times when you were successful at something, when you excelled at something and how you felt. Make sure the memory is fixed firmly in your mind and then intensify it.

Try to recall how it affected all of your senses. How did you feel? What did you hear? What did you see? Your goal is to create a powerful visual image in your mind, replaying every moment of that feel good experience so you can regenerate those same feelings again.

While that vivid impression is strong in your mind, think of one single word that will serve as a cue to help you to recall that experience each time you want to study. Make sure you breathe deeply as you do. Deep breathing takes in more oxygen, and more oxygen to the brain enhances your ability to learn.

Shut out all other memories except for that one and enjoy how it made you feel. Now, your mind is open, relaxed, and ready to embrace new information. You can also use this exercise to dispel any negative feelings that may come up that could interfere with your learning process.

Affirmations

Saying positive affirmations can be an amazing mood booster and a great aid in helping you to overcome any doubts you might be feeling. When tackling a new subject, we often feel unsure of ourselves. After all, we are entering a new territory.

Think of some positive affirmations to help describe how you're going to use your knowledge, how it is going to benefit you, and how well you will master your new subject. You can repeat these affirmations out loud or internally many times until your mind begins to believe it.

In the beginning, you may find this difficult to do. This is because of those preconceived negative feelings that we often have been led to believe. But, if you're isolated in your own private cocoon, then you will be more likely to say them until their results begin to take effect and you start to believe them. In here, repetition is the key. Say them often and repeatedly. These do not have to be attached to your study sessions. You can say them at any time when you need a mood booster. Say them when you first wake up in the morning, then maybe ten more times while you're having lunch, and several times throughout the day. The main point here is that the more often you say them, the easier it will be to believe them helping you to keep a positive frame of mind, which is conducive to quality study time.

Goals

Set clear goals for yourself. This way you can measure your learning progress. If you have no clear idea of why you're learning or what you want to accomplish, then it will be difficult for you to remain motivated and difficult to stay focused.

Try to visualize yourself after the learning is completed and you are applying it in your daily life. Practice the task or skill you are trying to learn in your mind before you even begin to use your hands. See yourself achieving the goals you've set for yourself.

Imagination

Another skill that children can do that adults generally try to beat it out of them is to use their imagination. This is not just mere child's play but has a very powerful effect on how well you learn. Imagination is much easier to do if you have passion for your subject. As Marilyn King of the **Dare to Imagine project** says, there are three things that all successful people have;

1. They are motivated.
2. They have clear-cut goals.
3. And they have vision. They can see themselves in action.

If your goals are specific and you are properly motivated, then your imagination will naturally follow. It's not enough to just say I want to do something, or I'm interested in it. You need to have a concrete plan where your learning sessions is pointing you towards.

Once you've done all of these things, you will be in the proper mental frame of mind to learn. When your mind is in gear and motivated properly, entering the learning phase will be much easier, and you'll be eager to devote yourself to study.

Step 2: Acquiring the Information

After you have placed your mind in gear, you are ready to start acquiring new knowledge. For most people, this stage represents the entire learning process. But as we've already discussed, it is only one phase.

Historically, acquiring knowledge has often been through reading, writing, and lecturing, which can only accommodate one type of learning. We live in a more advanced world now where in many cases you can pick and choose how you want to learn. For some people, learning in teams work best while for others, they may be happier if they were left to explore this new knowledge in their own time and at their own pace.

There are many ways you can start to absorb new information depending on your complement of intelligences, the amount of material you have to absorb, and the amount of time you have to dedicate to the learning process.

Speed Reading

Obviously, if you're in business and you need to absorb a lot of material to do your job well, you won't have the luxury of working at your own pace. In the business world, especially, this is often the case. The sheer quantity of information we must take in can sometimes seem overwhelming. We count the emails, reports, proposals, presentations, and websites we visit, and we might get discouraged before we get started.

We already understand that the best mental state for learning is relaxed and stress-free, but when we're faced with so much information to take in, it can be hard to make that happen. This is where speed reading can play a big role. By learning this simple technique, we can consume many times more information than normal and will be better able to keep up with the constant influx of data we need to absorb.

The average person reads at a rate of 250 words per minute but when you can master speed reading, you can easily double that rate and for some people, accomplish even more. To speed read successfully, in a way that will produce positive results, there are a few skills you will have to master.

There are several different approaches to speed reading, but one thing that they all emphasize is to turn off the little voice in your head that makes you "hear" the word as you're reading it. This is a skill you learn in school when you first learn to read. You start by mouthing the words, sounding out each one phonetically. As you become more proficient in reading through, you continue to do this action internally even though you have already mastered the skill and it is no longer needed. The problem with this is that we can voice and sound out words at a much slower pace than we can actually read. So by voicing those words, we are forcing our minds to slow down rather than to read at a speed closer to how fast we think.

The process is called sub-vocalization and if kept up, can severely slow down your ability to read fast. One way to train you to not do this is by learning to not look at a page one word at a time. Instead, see the written word as you might speak it. We don't speak one word at a time, but we speak with word groupings. You can do this by first relaxing your face and widening your focus on the page. Try placing the book further away from your eyes so that you can see entire lines at a time rather than individual words. Then you will begin to notice word patterns as your eyes skip from one spot to another. Scan your eyes down the center of the page allowing your peripheral vision to pick up the details that may be included at the end of each line.

This may seem a little strange to you, but once you've mastered it, you'll begin to see just how much faster your reading can be. This will allow you to absorb much more information in a shorter period of time so you can take in more knowledge at a faster rate. Below are several other speed reading techniques that can help you to consume knowledge faster.

The Pointer Method: The Pointer Method simply means that you run your finger along each line as you read. Instead of a finger, some people use a card under each line and slowly move it down the page as they read. It keeps you focused on where you are reading so your eyes don't jump lines and cause you to lose your place.

Tracker and Pacer Method: Similar to the Pointer Method, you can use a pen (cap on) and underline the lines as you read. Keep your eye trained just above the tip of the pen. It can help you improve your focus and maintain a steady pace as you read through each line. Set a goal to spend no more than one second per line and as you master that speed, you can start gradually increasing the speed until you reach your goal.

The Scanning Method: This method requires you to quickly move your eyes down the center of the page identifying specific keywords and phrases as you go. Here, look for key sentences that will help you to understand the context. Usually, these are the first sentence in each paragraph (topic sentences), important names, dates, numbers, or trigger words. You should rely heavily on your peripheral vision to pick up many important key points as you scan.

As you first practice these skills, you'll find you won't retain very much, but as you get more comfortable with this new style of reading, you'll find that your level of comprehension will naturally improve.

The Big Picture

As you begin to acquire information, it should be done in stages. One of the first things you want to do is get the big picture of your subject. Rather than focus on small details right off the bat, get a general overview of what you're about to learn. This is sort of like looking at the picture of a jigsaw puzzle before you put it together. You want to get a general idea of what you are about to take in.

Pay close attention to chapter titles, subheadings, examine any illustrations or auxiliary material that will help you to formulate a picture in your mind of what you're about to study.

The Core

Find the heart of the subject, the core idea. Once you understand the concepts, you're about to learn, things you read after that will make sense. What is it that you need to understand about this subject? Finding this small kernel of truth will help you to focus your mind on the fundamentals of the lesson and not get distracted by other details that may be interesting but not necessarily key to the main point of the lesson.

Small Bites

How do you eat an elephant? One bite at a time. Often when faced with massive amounts of material to take in, we can get discouraged before we begin. However, if you divide the material up into smaller manageable chunks, it will not feel so overwhelming. If you have to read a 600-page book, don't try to cram it all in at one time. Instead, break it up into smaller study periods, perhaps 25 pages at a time, or even 10. By taking it in one small section at a time, you'll be amazed at how fast you can accomplish this task.

Ask questions as you study. Fall in love with your 'WH' words. Who will benefit from this material? What does this mean? When did this happen? Where are we going?

Why are we doing it? How are we going to do it? Asking key questions keeps the mind engaged on the topic, so you are less likely to daydream or let your mind wander.

Tap Into Your Senses

Again, we want to remember to bring all the senses into it. One mother explained that she taught her son to read before he even started school by associating a sense of smell with each lesson. She would let him sniff a whiff of her perfume right before every lesson so that in time, he came to associate learning to read with the pleasant scent. In time he was to excel in nearly every subject he tried, learning hundreds of facts and figures in the process. Find creative ways to bring as many of the senses into play as you can. By doing this, you get the entire brain working at acquiring the knowledge and can keep you fully engaged for a longer period of time.

Learning Maps: Earlier in this book, we gave you an example of a learning map. Rather than taking notes in a linear way, creating learning maps engage the brain more in the learning process. It forces you to identify what the key points of your subject are and then spiral outward into more related topics.

In your learning map, make sure you use:

- Keywords
- Work from the main point outwards.
- Use lots of colors, pictures, and other triggers to help you remember.
- Make it as attractive and attention-grasping as possible.
- Make it in your iwn unique style.

By doing this, you not only are reviewing the information you're learning, but you're also identifying the key points, sifting through the data to glean information pertinent to your lesson, you're incorporating several different intelligences at the same time, and you're reinforcing the tools that will help you to remember better.

Frequency vs. Duration

When setting aside time to study, make sure that you focus on having shorter sessions more often. This will give your brain the rest it needs to sort through the information, giving you a better chance of remembering it.

Step 3: Searching Out the Meaning

Now that you have acquired the information, it is time to start analyzing it. This is where you will bring your inner child scientist out to play. Having knowledge is not the same thing as having understanding, and it is a far road from having wisdom. It is time to close your books or stop your mind from taking in more information and start to search for the deeper meaning behind the lessons.

Use Your Intelligences to Explore

This is where you can really have fun applying your eight intelligences to your study time. All of us have some intelligence that is more powerful than others, but you can even use your weaker intelligences to help you understand the meaning. You will benefit from this in two different ways. First, you will get more closely acquainted with your subject, and you will start to strengthen those intelligences that you may not have relied on too much in the past.

This will motivate you to think of the topic in different ways making you more creative and giving you a more open mind and approach to the subject. Test your knowledge out with each of these intelligences and start testing theories and answering the questions you formed in the previous step.

Take a Lesson from a Genius

If you've ever observed a person that is truly successful and has been for the better part of their lives, you will notice several habits that they all seem to have in common. They kept some type of daily journal, or they wrote extensively about their accomplishments to other people.

This practice started at a very early age, and it instilled discipline into their lives before they became successful. Thomas Edison for example, recorded something like three million pages of notes and letters throughout his lifetime.

These well-known men and women did not know that they were going to be famous or successful when they began writing, and they had no idea that anyone would even have the slightest interest in what they wrote down. While we may never know why these people became such prolific recorders, researcher Dr. Win Wenger concluded that these people were not born geniuses but used the writing as a means of nurturing and stimulating a growing body of knowledge.

Step 4: Triggering the Memory

At this point, you have only been able to master one half of the learning process. You have acquired the information, and you understand its meaning at its core. However, learning is only useful if you are able to recall it after you've acquired the knowledge. Without being able to remember the details of what you've learned, it will serve no useful purpose to you.

Throughout history, there have been records of people who have been able to recall several years' later details of what they have learned. These people have been studied repeatedly to find out what exactly makes it possible for them to recall data they acquired, sometimes many decades before.

The one thing that they all seemed to have in common was they had developed their own memory strategy. In this section, we will discuss some effective techniques and tricks designed to trigger the memory and compel your brain to give up the secrets it has stored. While these steps have proven effective, each person is different. Use the ones that work best for you, or may be enough to get you thinking about developing your own strategies. The main point here is that having a strategy is the key to helping you to recall the new lessons you've learned.

Seek Out the Unusual

When things are normal and constant, there is not enough stimulation to help us to recall it. However, when something appears out of the ordinary, your mind will naturally play closer attention to it. Your brain will create a vivid image of something that is out of place.

We naturally are drawn to things that are strange, unusual, funny, and even those things that are rude and offensive. So, when you learn something new, try to associate it with something out of the ordinary. Create a mental picture of it out of place. Try to enhance that image with an impractical story attached to it, and it will trigger your memory whenever the topic comes up.

A perfect example of this is the children's story that starts: *One dark night in the middle of the day two dead boys got up to fight...*

This type of exercise applied to your learning will keep the brain working on trying to make sense of the unusual parts of the story, and it will trigger memory recollection.

Organization

We also remember things better when they are given to us in an organized manner. Objects that are closely related will be stored in the same area of the brain. We naturally want to categorize things into different groups. Animals will all be associated with other animals in the same region or species. For example, when one person thinks of animals, they are probably going to recall the animals that they are most familiar with first. If you're from one region of the world, you'll think of dogs, cats, and birds, but if you're from another region, you're likely to think of giraffes, gazelles, and elephants. If you're down under, you're likely going to bring to mind dingos, hyenas, and wallabies.

When you organize what you're learning into easily discernible categories, the mind would probably trigger the first word on your list, and once that kicks in, the rest will follow.

Reality vs. Fantasy

It's much easier for the mind to recall real things rather than fantasy or make-believe. This does not mean that you can't recall a story, but instead, it refers to the idea that the image the knowledge produces is grounded in reality. We remember pictures and images much faster than we can recall the printed word. That's because we can relate to the visual imagery better than the image of the letters spread across the page.

Our visual imagery is much stronger than any of our other techniques. You recall that well-known expression - *A picture is worth a thousand words*. This is because our visual memory is an extremely powerful tool, especially when we incorporate colors, shapes, and angles in the imagery.

Associations

Linking what we learn to what we already know creates a strong foundation that can trigger our memory. By making associations that connect new knowledge to old, we literally can reinforce our minds and use already established memories as a trigger for the new knowledge.

Sleep

Many times, the reason we forget is that we never give our minds the time to process it. Without the processing time, our memories will simply fade much like the bright sunlight might bleach out the curtains on our windows. As we learned earlier, during the REM stage of sleep, the mind is sifting through everything we have learned in the day and making sense of it. This is the time when it is seared into our memories. However, if you're not getting enough rest, it is likely that you will have difficulty trying to recall the new information you've learned.

Action

There are numerous ways you can trigger your memory. Even when the material is complex, you need to create an action plan that will allow you to tap into these tools to help you recall the information. There are several steps to this type of action plan.

1. Make a conscious choice to remember.
2. Take plenty of breaks while you're learning.
3. Review the material during and after your study session.
4. Access your multi-sensory memories.

Acronyms

Almost every time you read study material, you'll see an acronym used to help you recall. We've even used a few of them in the pages of this book. An acronym is simply a word created by using the first letters of every word in a system or phrase. SCUBA for example: Self Contained Underwater Breathing Apparatus. Other acronyms you are already familiar with:

> FBI - Federal Bureau of
> Intelligence
> IRS - Internal Revenue Service
> USA - United States of America

The reason you see acronyms everywhere is that they work. If you're studying something that doesn't already have an acronym, then don't hesitate to create your own.

Flashcards

Some people find the use of flashcards very effective in remembering vocabulary and other single words or phrases. They work well when learning a foreign language and can be reviewed at almost any time. Flash cards can be mixed up rather than used in a particular order, allowing the brain to learn to process the information without creating a distinct pattern so it can mimic natural language better.

Repetition

Finally, try repetition. Each time you process the same information; the brain will see it as more important and begin to develop deeper connections as a result. Repetition is a key element in learning because it reinforces how the mind perceives it.

Step 5: Exhibiting What You Know

Parents often ask their children to tell them what they learned in school on that particular day. While they may not have realized it, they are teaching their children the art of repetition. This is not to recite the same phrases over and over again, but by having to explain what you have learned to someone else, you reinforce the lesson in your own mind.

This accomplishes two things. First, it lets you know if you truly understood the information and second it strengthens your knowledge of the subject internally.

Test

To make sure you really understand it, it is a good idea to test yourself on the subject. This could be done in any number of ways.

- Create a learning map
- Test yourself with flashcards
- Create a visual image of what you have learned
- Make a list
- Repeat it back to yourself (out loud)

By doing this, you will be able to identify when you've made a mistake, missed a point, or failed in some other way. That way, you can go back, review and correct them while you're still in the learning phase.

Practice

The only way to move from learner to expert in any area is with practice. There will always come a time when you have to put the book down and make practical application of your new knowledge. This is the only way it will become second nature to you. Whether you're into sports, learning a new language, or trying to master a new form of computer programming, practice is what will make you successful, not how much knowledge you've accumulated or how much time you've spent. Practice makes perfect.

Judge

Measure your success. This means to judge how well you've been able to achieve your goals. Mind you, this did not say to base this on a test someone else gives you. You should only be in competition with yourself, measuring your own level of progress. This will be more satisfying and rewarding to you than if you are judged based on what someone else may think you "should have" learned. Since we all acquire and process knowledge differently, measuring yourself against someone else would not reveal an honest picture of your progress nor would it do much in motivating you to continue.

Partner

Having a study partner has several benefits. They can serve as a sounding board as you try to mentally process the new information. You can bounce ideas off of them, role-play with them or even test each other.

Having a study partner also increases your accountability and motivation. It is easy to talk yourself out of studying when it is only you. But when you know someone else is counting on you, you are more inclined to work harder at it, knowing that someone else is depending on you.

If you don't have a study partner, use your family. Ask them to listen to your presentation, ask questions, and explain what you're working on - anything that they can do to help you to reinforce in your mind what you have learned.

Step 6: Reflection

The final stage of accelerated learning is to reflect back on the details that you've learned. A closer inspection on the steps you took to get there. Think about the steps you took that sped up the learning process and the things that got in your way. Consider alternative ways to reach the same conclusion.

A good review of not just what you've learned but the strategies and techniques you used to learn will automatically get your mind into an evaluation mode that will help you to firm up the new knowledge in your mind.

Personal Progress Plan

Consistent monitoring of your learning program will give you a clear picture of how well you are progressing and will reveal areas where you may need to adjust your approach. It's a good idea to keep a record of how you do, pinpointing areas where you may need to improve, and areas that you are doing well in.

If you find you are doing well, don't forget to reward yourself for your success.

Once you have mastered these six steps to accelerated learning, you will have built a strong foundation that will not only help you to acquire more knowledge but to do so in a way that you can more easily recall it when you need to.

Chapter 6: Alternative Learning

The methods for accelerated learning in the previous chapters are not the only means of speeding up the process. Researchers have been studying the human mind for centuries only to discover that there are a lot of different ways to master the art of acquiring new knowledge.

When deciding which of the following techniques work best for you, take a close look. Choose the ones that prove most effective. There were several commonalities that seemed to keep appearing.

Engaging the Mind

It cannot be emphasized enough that keeping the mind engaged is crucial to the learning process. Any method that stimulates the thought process, critical thinking and analysis will be very effective in boosting memory speed. When the mind is fully engaged, it is receptive to learning new knowledge. One is less likely to be distracted or to shut off mentally when the topic is able to keep us interested throughout the study session.

Even when there is not a strong interest in the subject, if the mind is engaged in problem-solving, strategizing, or analysis it will keep its attention for longer periods of time. Finding strategies that will do this is even more important in cases where the subject doesn't seem to be of any personal interest to the student.

Master the Concepts

Make sure that your alternative learning techniques also focus on mastering the concepts of the lesson you're studying. Before you start to focus on the minute little details, you need to get the main points of the lesson. These will act as a tether to your mind so that you can literally connect everything together.

The Wh - Cycle

To get a full body of knowledge, you want to make sure that you incorporate the Wh-Cycle or the question phase of the lesson. No lesson is complete until it has answered all of the wh-questions.

You've probably been around a lot of small children and have experienced being on the other end of their inquisitiveness. The "why" phase that all little ones go through starts with a basic question about something and then is followed by an endless stream of whys. These children are relentless and will not stop until the adults give up or they get a definitive answer to their questions.

You need to be in that same mental state of mind in your approach to study. The subject may seem frustrating and boring but if you've genuinely engaged your mind, searching for the answers won't seem like tedious work but will give you a feeling of satisfaction that you have looked under every stone for the practical solutions to every problem.

The only difference is that your questions will take on a more detailed approach. Create questions that will help you to solve a problem, develop a skill or talent or even create the necessary connections you need to meet your objectives.

This method is simple and can be applied to any topic. You will find that the more you build on your knowledge, the more questions you will have. Asking these types of questions will not only reinforce what you already know but help you to establish a strong foundation for further learning in the future.

Convince Yourself

Develop arguments that require you to defend a position. This means that you will first have to convince yourself that your conclusions drawn about your lessons are accurate. Practice explaining this lesson to yourself, or teaching yourself how to solve problems and bring them to a satisfactory conclusion.

This technique is actually an extension of the Wh-cycle whereas the Wh-cycle concentrates on getting to the core of a topic, asking the who, what, when, where, and whys of a matter. When you try to convince yourself of a particular solution, you are more likely to focus more on the "how" of the matter; you want to know the manner in which something is done.

This is the phase of review where you will get into more specific details and focus more on solving problems or addressing issues.

It helps to do this phase of the work verbally. It will add an auditory element to your learning.

1. Identify the problem.
2. Develop several solutions.

3. Analyze the potential results.
4. Come up with a viable answer.

This step will confirm if you really understand the subject matter. It lets you know if you need to go back again to pick up points that you missed.

The Feynman Technique: One successful way to convince yourself is by applying the Feynman technique in your self-analysis. Named after a physicist by the name of Richard Feynman, this technique has four steps:

1. Choose a concept.
2. Record an explanation in simple English.
3. Find your blind spots - areas where your knowledge and understanding are weak.
4. Create an analogy to explain it.

The fourth step is the primary means of creating a connection between all the new information you've accumulated and binds it with the old knowledge you have already acquired. This four-step process makes sure that you not only know your topic well but that you can quickly identify where you need more work, so you finish with a very solid base of knowledge.

Interleaved Practice

Blocking is a strategy that allows you to focus on one single skill at a time and gradually build on that until you reach your goal. It is more often used when you're trying to learn multiple skills all working towards the same goal. In other words, you need to be able to perform a task that incorporates five different skills. Your initial study periods will be trained on mastering Skill A and nothing else. Once you are comfortable with Skill A, then you move on to Skill B, then Skill C, then D, and finally Skill E. The goal is to completely master one skill first before moving on to the next one.

Interleaving, however, pulls you away from this traditional style of learning in sequence. It mixes the skills up in such a way that you are tackling all the skills at the same time. So, rather than the logical approach of ABCDE, you might have an approach that looks more like ABCDE-ABCDE-ABCDE-ABCDE.

This approach may appear to be chaotic, however, so remember what we said in a previous chapter about taking things in smaller bites. Research supports this approach as it is more closely linked to how we absorb things in real life. We don't naturally learn things in a perfect, orderly fashion but it's thrown at us all at once. As a result, interleaved practice is more in line with how our brains really absorb the details we need to learn.

Chapter 7: Reinforce

The final step in accelerated learning is to reinforce what you have learned. Your brain is like a muscle. It is continuously building pathways throughout your life in a similar way to how muscles can build up tissue. However, those pathways will fade if they are not exercised, just like your muscles will begin to get flabby if not worked on a regular basis.

It's important to keep your mind active throughout your lives. Education should not be limited to only young minds but is a necessity for all age groups. It is not enough to study something one time, and you will know it for life. You have to reinforce it by studying it again but from a different angle.

The more you engage your complete brain in the learning process the stronger your pathways will be. So, if the first time you pick it up you learn it visually then the second time you might want to think about learning using an auditory medium, kinesthetic, or interpersonal.

Embrace Your Mistakes

It bears repeating - mistakes are going to happen no matter what you do. Regardless of how hard you study or how much effort you put into it, you will hit a few snags that will catch you up here and there. You need to view these bumps in the road like a small child learning how to walk. It does not matter how other people view your mistakes or errors, it's what you do with them.

Losses are Not Failures: The fact that you won't get it right every time should not discourage you. Losses do not represent failure on your part. Once you view this as a point where your mind needs to be readjusted, you take away the negativity that seems to be a knee-jerk reaction when one makes a mistake.

Learn how to embrace your mistakes so that you can use them to enhance your education rather than to demonstrate that you haven't met some pre-established standard that you have not yet met.

Build Expertise

Remember, our goal for learning is to build expertise or skill in a given area. Learning is not there for the sake of creating an impressive repertoire of knowledge that you can showcase for other people. While you could do that, if your goal is more in line with finding ways to use the knowledge to the advantage of yourself or your employer, you will get a lot more satisfaction from what you are gaining.

There are a few basic guidelines you can follow until you reach a point where you can be considered an expert at anything. Follow these steps, and you'll be well on your way.

10,000 Hours: This rule can apply to just about any skill or talent you are hoping to develop. No matter what it is, expect that you will spend lots of hours of study and more importantly, practice in order to become proficient. Then you will not only perform like an expert but actually begin to believe in your expertise in your own right.

Practice: You can't reach those 10,000 hours without regular practice of your new information. Your practice sessions should be deliberate and consistent. Regular practice, whether it is in sports, in music, or any other endeavor will embed this knowledge so deeply in your brain it will become second nature to you.

The 80/20 Rule: The basic principle is that of all the things you do in life, only 20% of it is really going to matter in the grander scheme of things. This rule has consistently proved true through many years.

- In business - 80% of sales come from 20% of customers
- In work environments - 80% of results come from 20% of the workers
- Relationships: 80% of happiness comes from 20% of relationships

By focusing your study on the 20% that which truly matters and is important, you won't waste a lot of time on insignificant information that won't help you to reach your goals.

Teach Someone Else

The ability to have a front row seat into how other people's brains work gives you a privileged view into how to assimilate information. Because every brain is different, we all absorb information in a different way. There is nothing more inspiring than watching the light bulb go on in someone's eyes when they finally understand something. The light in their face is something that has no other equal in this universe.

By teaching others you not only reinforce your own knowledge of the subject, but it also opens your minds to additional ways to gather information. You get to share both student and teacher experiences that will only compound your own knowledge. If you are lucky enough to have someone you can share your knowledge with, here are a few pointers that will help you to not only be an accelerated learner but a highly efficient teacher at the same time.

The Learning Pyramid: Sometimes referred to as the "cone of experience," the learning pyramid is a tool that helps us to understand why teaching can be such an important part of the learning process. The stats below make it clear why we should focus our energies on more quality learning.

- 90% of what we learn, we retain when we teach someone else, or we use it immediately.
- 75% of what we learn is reinforced when practiced.
- 50% is retained when engaged in open discussion.
- 30% is retained when they observe a visual demonstration.
- 20% is retained when they receive an auditory lesson.
- 10% is retained from what we read.

- 5% is retained from what we hear (lectures).

Since there are no tests that actually "prove" these statistics, the learning pyramid has its own share of opponents. However, it does reinforce the general idea that the more involved you are in the learning process, the faster and the easier it will be to acquire the knowledge.

It doesn't matter if you totally agree with the numbers or not, it is clear that even if you view this information as an estimate of the learning process, teaching others is the most involved of all aspects of learning strategies and the more engaged you are, the more you will learn and remember. Unlike the more passive learning practices, teaching others cements the lessons firmly in the mind and forces you to see what you have truly accomplished.

This is because you are forced to show your knowledge and explain it in a way that will help others. When others are relying on what you know, you cannot make generalizations, skip steps, or avoid areas that you may feel are too difficult. You have to have every detail clear in your mind and are prepared to answer questions as others will.

It also has an effect on your motivation to learn. When you know that others are depending on you to give them quality knowledge, you are more likely to work harder to make sure that you understand the material and know how to use it accurately. For this reason, students who tutor others generally fare much better than those students who do not. There are three primary reasons why this has been so effective.

1. It gives you, the teacher, permission to look at your failures without any negative feelings associated with them. Your motivations are more to help your student rather than to feel bad about your own shortcomings.

2. It forces you to analyze your own way of understanding. You review and revise your own view as you witness how your line of thinking impacts another person.

3. It adds a higher level of responsibility to learning. With more responsibility, you are more inclined to take your learning seriously. When you realize that what you say and do will have an effect on someone else, you will be more meticulous about making sure that the information you teach is correct from the beginning.

As we teach others though, it is important that you make sure the other person is engaged in the learning process. Avoid the tendency to start lecturing your students. While some may be able to gather some knowledge, this is a more passive approach for the student, which will only lead to a decline in their ability to absorb the information.

To that end, there is another level of knowledge you must acquire to become an effective teacher or tutor. You need to also understand your student. So, in addition to dispensing information about your topic, you once again become a student as you learn more about your student and what they really need.

This type of information is most likely gained by asking strategic questions. You need to know the same things about your student as you needed to understand about yourself when you started learning. This will help to sharpen your focus on demonstrating what they need, filling in the gaps, and trying to dispense information from a completely different perspective. There are seven different types of questions that will give you a good gauge on what your student needs and how you can tailor your lessons to meet them.

1. What's on your mind: This encourages the student to address their own problem or to look inside to find out what they really need to know.

2. What else do you want to know: This forces the student to look deeper at their situation and get to the core of what they hope to achieve from their lesson.

3. What are your challenges: This question forces the student to analyze their own abilities, levels of concentration, and perceptions of the subject. In essence, they compare their approach to learning to themselves but not in comparison with others.

4. What do you want: What do they hope to gain from the lesson? It helps you to see what their motivation for learning really is; what's in their heart.

5. How can I help: By now you probably have a good idea of what you can do to help this student, but here you can gather what the student thinks would be the right solution. You will learn what they expect to get from you during the lesson. It will make it clear what is really important to the student.

6. What are you saying no to: Every time a student agrees to study with you, he's making a choice; by choosing you, they are saying no to something else they could be doing. So find out what they are declining in order to learn from

you. You'll learn what sacrifices they are making to gain a piece of your knowledge.

7. What was most helpful for you: This question is in the past tense since you will ask it after your lesson with the student. It is a way of getting them to review their lesson and discover what new things they have learned. It establishes a value for your lesson and highlights for both of you how it has benefitted them in some way.

Finally, you want to make sure that you give good feedback; something that will help the student to grow. When you teach, you take the whole concept and break it down into small bite-sized pieces that will help to enhance the student's comprehension. Your feedback is a key to preparing the next lesson. You will give honest but encouraging help here that will teach them to focus on the areas they are weak in.

Make sure that your feedback is very specific as it will tell them exactly what they need to know. Don't hesitate to give it, the sooner you give it, the sooner the student can start making changes. Make sure they have a goal. It gives them something to ground them and a focus to aim for. And finally, give it in a way that makes them want to come back to you for more. If your words are harsh and insensitive, they may develop a fear of learning. But if you offer encouragement and practical assistance that will move them forward, then you will instill confidence and motivate them to want to learn more.

Give them a plan of action. This will serve as a blueprint of steps they can take that will help them to move forward. Don't just tell them "work on this" or "work on that" without giving them some guidelines to follow. It will instill trust in you as a teacher, and help them to be more optimistic about their studies.

Finally, you want your student to give you feedback to show you how you can improve your teaching methods. Encourage them to be honest with you about how you teach. Students may be hesitant at first to give you their opinions, but the more often you ask, their barriers will begin to come down, and they will give you the kind of information that will not only ensure that you are an effective teacher but an excellent student as well.

Conclusion

Thank for making it through to the end of *Accelerated Learning Crash Course.* Let's hope it was informative and able to provide you with all of the tools you need to achieve your goals whatever they may be.

It doesn't matter if we are educators, business executives, government officials, students, or parents. We all need to become better learners if we hope to keep up with this fast paced life. We need to completely change our view of what is involved in the learning process and our approach to it.

It needs to be something that is as natural to us as eating; something that we can do at every stage of our lives and will never stop doing. For this, we have to be as innocent as babies when we first enter the world, full of curiosity and dreams.

By finding your inner child and bringing him out of hiding, you will be able to access more of your brain power, utilize your many forms of intelligence, build on existing knowledge, and increase your learning potential by leaps and bounds.

Just as a review, through these pages we've learned:

- Learning is for everyone regardless of age or position in life.

- Accelerated learning is necessary for the faster and more technologically advanced world we live in.

- How to prepare your mind and heart to learn.

- The importance of strengthening the memory when you learn.

- How the brain really works and how to best access it.

- How to use your multiple intelligences to enhance learning.

- How to use emotions while learning.

- The Six Steps to Faster Learning

- How to seal in the knowledge so you can access it later.

- And so much more

If you are truly committed to faster learning, then we hope that the guidelines we offer in this book will be of extreme value to you. Once you master them and apply them in your daily life, you should see phenomenal success in absorbing new information at a much faster rate.

Lightning Source UK Ltd.
Milton Keynes UK
UKHW021111180821
389055UK00012B/819